COOKING WILD

TAKING YOUR HARVEST FROM FIELD TO TABLE

JOHN McATEER

PUBLISHED BY FIDELI PUBLISHING, INC.

ISBN: 978-1-955622-92-9

Note: Photos may not exactly represent what each recipe will look
like when prepared.

Published by

Fideli Publishing, Inc.
119 W. Morgan St.
Martinsville, IN 46151

www.FideliPublishing.com

I would like to take a moment to dedicate my cook book to all the sportsman and ladies who enjoy the great outdoors. To all the dark, unknown trails that have given me my greatest challenges, and most of all to all of God's wonderful creatures.

Remember, conservation is not only a word, it's a way of life. If we protect nature, our story will live on thru the eyes of a new generations.

TABLE OF CONTENTS

INTRODUCTION

I have been fortunate to have been able to travel the globe pursuing many great adventures in the Wild Outdoors. I faced many challenges along the way, and never take for granted how lucky I have been. I also never want to waste the bounty provided by the animals I harvest and make sure each animal I harvest is used fully.

I hope these recipes allow you to go wild with your cooking as you bring your game from Field to Table.

Bon appétit!

WHITE-TAILED DEER

My first hunt started on a crisp, clear October morning in 1970 and ended with a bow shot that gave me my first buck and my first trophy, an eight-point Whitetail buck.

Eight-point Whitetail buck, harvested in October in New York.

White-Tailed Deer Loaf

INGREDIENTS

1-1/2 lb shoulder of venison

3 or 4 slices of day-old
    bread made into 1-1/3
    cups loosely packed
    bread crumbs

3 T of finely chopped celery

3 T butter

1 cup water

1 medium bay leaf

Marrow

1-1/4 tsp salt

1/4 to 1/2 tsp marjoram
    (optional)

1-1/2 tsp onion, grated

1 egg, slightly beaten

INSTRUCTIONS

Wipe meat with a clean, damp cloth and trim off any tough tissue or strong-smelling fat. Remove bones and grind meat. There should be 1 lb of ground meat when you're done. Save marrow.

Tear the slices of bread into small crumbs or pulse in food processor. Sauté celery in butter for 5 minutes; add water, bay leaf and simmer 3 minutes. Discard bay leaf. Combine cooled liquid with crumbs; add meat, marrow and remaining ingredients. Mix thoroughly.

Turn into a greased loaf pan (3-3/4 x 7-1/2 inches) and bake in a moderate oven (350° F) for 1 hour.

Serves 6.

NOTE: *When cooking white-tailed deer, you need to remember that it has a characteristically gamey flavor, although it is lighter in taste than say the mule deer. The taste is also dependent on the deer's diet. This animal's meat is one of the healthiest out there.*

TIP: *If you're concerned about a gamey taste, many hunters that swear by dairy products when it comes to removing gaminess as dairy "bleeds out" many meats, with blood being a source of gamey flavor. Soak the meat in dairy before preparing any recipe.*

Barbecued White-Tailed Deer Tenderloin

INGREDIENTS

1 deer tenderloin (1-1/4 lb.) 2 T butter or shortening

SAUCE INGREDIENTS:

1 cup catchup
2 T onion, grated
1/2 cup celery, chopped
1/2 cup water
2 tsp vinegar
1-1/2 tsp salt

1/4 to 1/2 tsp
   Worcestershire (to taste)
Kick it up a bit by adding
   jalapeños or Tabasco
   sauce to taste

INSTRUCTIONS

Cut tenderloin into slices 1-3/4-inch thick (makes about 6). Trim off any strong fat or tough membrane.

Heat butter in a skillet and brown slices of deer quickly.

Meanwhile, combine remaining ingredients and pour over hot meat. Place uncovered in a moderate oven (350° F) for 1 hour.

Baste meat occasionally with the barbecue sauce and turn once during baking time.

Serves 6.

SERVING SUGGESTION:

This venison dish goes well with garlic mashed potatoes.

GARLIC MASHED POTATOES

INGREDIENTS

8 large red potatoes, peeled and quartered
1/2 cup milk
4 T butter

2 cloves garlic, minced
salt to taste
1 pinch ground white pepper

INSTRUCTIONS

Bring a large pot of water to boil; add potatoes, and boil until soft, about 20–25 minutes. Drain, and place in a large bowl.

Combine potatoes with milk, butter, garlic, salt, and pepper and mix with an electric mixer or potato masher to your desired consistency.

WHITE-TAILED DEER GOULASH

INGREDIENTS

2 lb leg of venison, cut into 2-inch chunks

1 T white wine vinegar

1/2 lb smoked bacon, finely chopped

1 large yellow onion, finely chopped

1-1/2 T hot paprika, preferably Hungarian

1/4 tsp dried ground thyme

1/4 tsp dry mustard

4 whole allspice berries

4 juniper berries

2 cloves garlic, finely chopped

1 small tomato, cored and chopped

1/2 green bell pepper, cored, seeded and finely chopped

1 cup red wine, preferably merlot

Salt

Freshly ground black pepper

INSTRUCTIONS

Put venison and vinegar in a bowl and cover with boiling water.

Cook bacon until crisp in a large pot over medium heat, 6-8 minutes. Add onions and cook until softened, 6-8 minutes.

Drain venison, add to onions and cook over medium-high heat until just browned, 8-10 minutes.

Stir in 1 cup water, paprika, thyme, mustard, allspice, juniper, garlic, tomatoes, and peppers and reduce heat to medium-low.

Cover and simmer until venison is just tender, about 2 hours.

Uncover pot, add wine and salt to taste. Continue cooking until venison is very tender and liquid has thickened, about 1-1/2 hours.

Serve with parsley potatoes and crusty bread.

BLACK BEAR

To find this Black Bear, I traveled to Québec in early June. I harvested this animal with my Black Eagle. His live weight was approximately 200 lbs, and I was careful to preserve his hide when capping him out. I would recommend bear hunting to all sportsmen and sportswomen. It's thrilling and unpredictable and, like many other hunting endeavors, rewarding.

Bear Loin Steaks

INGREDIENTS

2 loin steaks, 2-1/2 lbs, 5/8-
   to 3/4-inch thick*
1 T butter,
   melted

2 tsp lemon juice
1-1/4 tsp salt
Generous dash of pepper
1/2 cup boiling water

INSTRUCTIONS

Wipe steaks clean with a damp cloth. Trim off all the fat because it has a strong flavor. This should leave about 1-1/2 lbs lean steak.

Place steak on a hot, greased broiler rack set 4 inches from heat. Combine butter and lemon juice and brush over top of steaks. Sprinkle with half of the salt and pepper. Broil 7 to 8 minutes.

Turn steaks, brush with remaining lemon-butter and remaining salt and pepper. Broil another 7 or 8 minutes for well-done steaks.

Remove from broiler to platter. Drizzle 1/2 cup water over rack and scrape down the residue into the drip pan. Remove rack. Stir gravy until well blended, reheat to boiling. Pour over hot steaks and serve immediately.

Serves 4 to 5.

*If the steaks seem tough, the meat may be pounded or diced as in preparation for cubed steak.

TIP: The internal temperature of cooked bear meat must reach 160° and stay there for a minimum of three minutes. Never eat pink meat and there should be no pink juice dripping from the meat.

When cooking bear meat with bones, be aware that bones absorb heat and slow the cooking process, so be sure to check the meat around the bone to be sure it's done before you serve it.

Bear Stew

INGREDIENTS

4 lbs bear meat, cubed
1/4 cup all-purpose flour
1 tsp dried oregano
1 tsp salt
1 tsp ground black pepper
4 T butter
2 T olive oil
1 onion, chopped

1 cup beef broth
4 bay leaves
2 lbs red potatoes, diced
1 pound fresh mushrooms
5 carrots, sliced
2 turnips, cubed

INSTRUCTIONS

In a large mixing bowl combine flour, oregano, salt and pepper. Place bear meat in the bowl a little at a time and coat well.

Heat oil and butter in a large skillet. Fry the bear meat until browned. Let drain on paper towels.

Fill a large Dutch oven with 2 to 3 quarts water. Add bear meat, onions, beef broth, bay leaves, potatoes, mushrooms carrots and turnips.

Cook on medium-high heat for 2 to 3 hours. Add more water as needed.

Natural ground blind.

I prefer a ground blind to a tree stand. I usually set my blind within 20 yards of the baited area, depending upon wind direction. I like this method better because I feel it puts me on the same level as the bear.

SAUERBRATEN STYLE BEAR

INGREDIENTS

1 4-pound bear roast
1-1/2 cup red wine
1 cup red wine vinegar
2 onions, 1 grated, 1
   chopped)
1 carrot, chopped
1 stalk celery, chopped
6 juniper berries
4 bay leaves
4 cloves

1 T black peppercorns
Kosher salt
3 T bacon fat
2 T butter
2 T flour
1 T sugar
1/4 cup golden raisins
1/4 cup chopped parsley

Simmer red wine, vinegar, grated onion, carrot and celery in a Dutch oven over medium-high heat.

Tie juniper berries, bay leaves, cloves and peppercorns in cheesecloth bundle (bouquet garni) and add to the pot. Remove from the heat and let cool completely before pouring over the bear roast. Marinate for 24 hours minimum.

Remove the bear from marinade and pat dry with paper towels. Sprinkle liberally with kosher salt and let rest.

Heat bacon fat in a Dutch oven and sauté chopped onions until translucent, about 3–4 minutes. Add the bear and brown on all sides.

Strain the marinade through a fine sieve and add that liquid to the Dutch oven. Bring to a heavy simmer, and cover.

Braise in 325° F. oven for 2-1/2–3 hours, or until the roast is very tender, but not falling apart.

Transfer the bear roast to a platter. Strain remaining liquid and reserve.

Melt butter in the Dutch oven and stir in the flour and sugar to make a roux. Cook, stirring, for 2–3 minutes then whisk in the reserved liquid. Add golden raisins and simmer until gravy has slightly thickened.

To serve, cut the bear into thick slices and pour gravy over it, then sprinkle with chopped parsley.

Pairs nicely with traditional German dumplings, potatoes spaetzle or red cabbage.

WYOMING ANTELOPE

I visited my friend Jerry Matthews in Wyoming to hunt antelope hunt. It was a hot day, 96 degrees by noon, when I finally had a 40-yard broadside shot at this beautiful animal that was a fine representation of an antelope and quite a prize, harvested in Casper, Wyoming.

Braised Antelope Chops in Mushroom Gravy

INGREDIENTS

4 good-sized loin chops
   (weight about 1-1/2 lbs)
1-3/4 tsp salt
Pinch of pepper
3 T butter
1 cup water

10-1/2 oz can mushroom
   soup
1 tsp sherry
Tabasco or other hot sauce
   to taste

INSTRUCTIONS

Wipe chops clean with a damp cloth and trim off any strong-smelling fat. Sprinkle chops with salt and pepper.

Use a skillet with tight-fitting cover to brown chops slowly (uncovered) on both sides in heated butter. Add 1/4 cup of water, cover and simmer 15 minutes, then add 1/4 cup more water and again cover and simmer 15 minutes.

Next, add the rest of the water and the soup. Cover and continue cooking very slowly for half an hour. Last, add sherry and Tabasco sauce. Serve with crispy garlic potatoes.

CRISPY GARLIC POTATOES

INGREDIENTS

2 lbs potatoes, cut into 1-inch cubes
2 T olive oil
1 tsp sea salt

3/4 tsp freshly ground black pepper
2 T garlic, minced
2 T fresh chopped parsley

Preheat the oven to 400° F.

Lightly spray a baking sheet or tray with cooking oil spray and arrange potatoes on in single layer.

Drizzle with oil and season with salt, pepper and garlic. Toss so potatoes are evenly coated.

Roast for 45-55 minutes while flipping occasionally, until crisp and golden.

Remove from oven and season with a little extra salt and pepper to taste. Sprinkle with parsley and serve.

Antelope Goulash

INGREDIENTS

1 T butter

1 lb antelope meat, ground

1/4 cup green bell pepper, chopped

1/4 cup onion, chopped

2 T fresh chives, chopped

1 15.25-oz can whole kernel corn, drained

2 red potatoes, cubed

1 tomato, chopped

1 stalk celery, finely chopped

3 14-oz cans beef broth

1 cup water

1 cup elbow macaroni

Salt and black pepper to taste

1/4 tsp garlic powder, or to taste

INSTRUCTIONS

Stir butter, antelope, bell pepper, onion, and chives together in a large pot over medium heat until the vegetables are very tender and the antelope has browned, about 10 minutes.

Stir in the corn, red potatoes, celery, tomato, beef broth, water, and macaroni. Bring to a boil over high heat; reduce heat to medium-low, cover, and simmer until the potatoes are tender, about 30 minutes.

Season to taste with salt, pepper, and garlic powder before serving.

Sweet and Spicy Antelope with Mushrooms

INGREDIENTS

Antelope backstrap, sliced
    into 1/4-inch pieces

1/4 tsp garlic powder

1/4 tsp cumin

1/4 tsp turmeric

3-4 T butter

2 T mango chutney

1/4 cup sweet onion, sliced

4 Portobelo mushrooms,
    sliced

1-2 Thai red and green chilis
    (the more the better, if
    you like spicy), diced

Thai basil, parsley or chives
    for garnish

INSTRUCTIONS

Cut antelope backstrap into eight 1/2-inch thick pieces. In separate bowl, mix garlic powder, cumin and turmeric together and rub on both sides of the antelope pieces. Set meat aside.

Heat cast iron skillet on medium-high heat. Melt butter and add onion and mushrooms. Cook until onions become translucent, 5-8 minutes. Add chutney and Thai chilis and stir. Move to the side of the pan.

Add meat to the same pan and cook for 1-2 minutes, then turn and cook other side for 1 minute. (This will ensure that the antelope remains tender and flavorful.)

Stir antelope into mushrooms and onions. Remove to platter and garnish with fresh Thai basil or chives.

When hunting antelope with a bow and arrow, one usually hunts over a watering hole, which may be hot and boring at times. An average antelope may only go to a watering hole once or twice a day.

MOUNTAIN CARIBOU

This quest for mountain caribou sent me to British Columbia, where I worked with a fantastic outfitter, Love Bros. & Lee. I brought my dependable Fred Bear Polar LTD bow along for this hunt. I harvested the caribou on day four of a five-day hunt.

Caribou Stroganoff

INGREDIENTS

1-1/2 lb Caribou steak or
    boneless stewing meat,
    cut in 1/2 inch strips
1/2 cup flour
1/2 tsp salt
1/2 lb mushrooms, sliced
1 large onion, chopped
1 clove garlic, minced

3 T lard or bacon fat
1 T Worcestershire sauce
1 beef bouillon cube
1 cup water
1 cup sour cream
noodles or steamed rice
paprika (optional)

INSTRUCTIONS

Pound meat to tenderize if needed, though good quality steaks will not need this. (You can also use ground meat.)

Mix 1/4 cup flour with salt and dredge meat. In a large skillet, sauté garlic, onions and mushrooms in fat for 5 minutes. Remove them, add meat and brown. Remove meat from pan.

Dissolve bullion cube in water. Add remaining flour to drippings in pan and stir. Add Worcestershire and the dissolved bouillon. Cook until thickened.

Add sour cream. Heat until gravy simmers, then add the meat and vegetables and heat. Serve over rice or noodles. Sprinkle with paprika to garnish.

INTERESTING MOUNTAIN CARIBOU FACTS

- Caribou survived the Pleistocene Ice Age extinctions that erased mammoths, mastodons, short-faced bears, ice-age camels, and many others after making their way to North America over the Bering Land Bridge thousands of years ago.

- Mountain caribou are larger than deer and smaller than elk, with males weighing approximately 175 kg. Their hollow fur insulates them through the long mountain winters. Caribou are unique in the deer family in that both females and males grow antlers.

- Unique behavior allows mountain caribou to live where other ungulates cannot survive.

Cherry Caribou Tenderloin

INGREDIENTS

1 Caribou tenderloin
1 tsp salt
Pinch of pepper to taste
3 T unsalted butter
1/4 cup shallots, sliced
1/4 cup red peppers, sliced

1/4 cup zucchini, sliced to mimic peppers
1/2 cup aged Balsamic vinegar
1/2 cup cherry preserves

INSTRUCTIONS

Season tenderloin with salt and pepper. Melt butter in a skillet and sear meat on both sides until medium rare, then let it rest.

In a small skillet add 1 T butter and sliced vegetables. Sauté 3 minutes. Add pepper, salt, vinegar and cherry preserves and sauté until sauce slightly thickens. Add remaining butter to sauce and stir.

Slice tenderloin thin, place on top of vegetables and pour sauce over all.

GRILLED MARINATED CARIBOU SIRLOIN

INGREDIENTS

2-1/2 cups Caribou sirloin, trimmed and cut into 2-inch cubes
3/4 cup olive oil
1/2 cup honey
1/4 cup red wine vinegar
1 T garlic powder

1/3 cup low-sodium soy sauce
1-1/2 tsp ground ginger
1-1/2 tsp kosher salt
1 T freshly ground black pepper

INSTRUCTIONS

Combine all ingredients aside from caribou into a tight-fitting jar and shake vigorously. Can be stored in the refrigerator for several weeks.

Place caribou in a non-reactive container or zip-lock bag. Add marinade, toss and refrigerate for 1-6 hours.

When ready to cook, remove from marinade, drain and place on a medium-high, well-oiled grill and brown on all sides, preferably not past medium-rare (130-135°F internal temperature).

Serves 4.

Caribou Meatballs in Onion Gravy

INGREDIENTS

1-1/2 lb Caribou shoulder
1-1/4 cup bread crumbs, loosely packed
1/2 cup celery, finely chopped
1/3 cup butter
Marrow, if any

1 large egg, slightly beaten
1/2 cup water
1-1/2 tsp salt
Generous dash pepper
1/2 tsp poultry seasoning
noodles of your choice

INSTRUCTIONS

Wipe meat with a clean damp cloth, trim off any strong smelling fat and remove bones. Grind meat twice. Reserve any marrow.

Sauté celery in 2 T of butter for 10 minutes, then add to meat along with bread crumbs, marrow and the remaining ingredients except butter. Mix thoroughly.

Shape into small meatballs about 1 inch in diameter. Brown in the remaining butter quickly; lower heat and cook over medium heat for 10 minutes.

Add onion gravy and simmer 2 minutes. Makes 3 to 3-1/2 dozen small meatballs. Serve with gravy and seasoned fries.

ONION GRAVY

INGREDIENTS

1-1/2 T flour
2 T butter
1 cup water
1/2 tsp salt

1 cup (2 medium) red onions, thinly sliced
1 cup lettuce, finely shredded

INSTRUCTIONS

Combine flour and melted butter in a skillet and stir over medium heat until mixture is browned (not scorched); add water gradually and cook until mixture is smooth and thick; stir constantly. Add remaining ingredients, cover and simmer for 15 minutes.

Caribou Stew Deluxe

MARINADE INGREDIENTS:

2 cups red wine (Burgundy
   or Claret)
1/4 cup cider vinegar
2 juniper berries, cut in
   fourths
1 tsp salt

1/4 tsp whole black pepper
1 medium bay leaf
1/2 medium onion, sliced
1/2 small carrot, sliced
2 whole cloves of garlic,
   crushed

STEW INGREDIENTS:

2-1/2 lb Caribou shoulder
3 T shortening
1/2 tsp pepper
1-1/8 tsp salt

1 medium onion, sliced
1/2 cup tomato purée
3/4 cup water
1 T flour

INSTRUCTIONS

Wipe meat with a clean damp cloth, trim off any strong smelling fat, then cut into two-inch cubes. Place in a glass or enamelware pan or bowl and pour the cold marinate over the meat. Turn the meat in the marinade twice daily. Marinate at least 24 hours, going longer for richer flavor.

When ready to cook, lift the meat out to drain on paper towel to prevent too much splattering when browning. Heat shortening in an aluminum kettle or skillet (iron may give a dark color) and brown the meat slowly on all sides. Add 3/4 cup of the strained marinade, pepper and salt. Cover and simmer gently for 1-1/2 hours. Then add onion, tomatoes and 1/2 cup water and continue to simmer for another hour. Thicken the sauce with flour blended into a smooth paste in remaining 1/4 cup of water. Boil 2 minutes longer.

One of two Québec-Labrador Caribou harvested in Schefferville, Québec, Canada. Both made Pope & Young.

UTAH MOUNTAIN LION

I trained hard for the trip to the Book Cliff Mountains in Utah with Jerry Borden and it paid off for me in a big way! The Mountain Lion harvested in Book Cliff Mountains in Utah was the biggest and oldest the Colorado Fish & Wildlife Conservation Office had ever recorded. It ended up being the number-one lion in the state that year, It scored a 16 inches green score, made Pope & Young and was eligible for Boone and Crockett as well.

MOUNTAIN LION MEATBALLS STUFFED WITH CHEESE

2-1/2 cups Mountain Lion, trimmed and cut into 2-inch cubes
3/4 cup olive oil
1/2 cup honey
1/4 cup red wine vinegar
1 T garlic powder
1-1/2 tsp ground ginger

1/3 cup low-sodium soy sauce
1-1/2 tsp kosher salt
1 T freshly ground black pepper
1/2 cup Panko bread crumbs

INSTRUCTIONS

Mix meat with all ingredients except cheese and oil. Make small balls of the mixture, then insert a piece of cheese inside each.

Refrigerate for one hour minimum.

Roll each meatball in Panko until coated.

Pour oil into a frying pan and heat it until oil shimmers. Drop meatballs into oil one by one and fry until they are brown and crisp.

THE REST OF THE STORY...

Two years after this epic hunt, my good friend Jerry Boren passed away, leaving a massive hole in my heart. I will always recall the smile on Jerry's face when we harvested that enormous old cat. Giants are not measured by their size but rather by how they affect your life, and Jerry certainly was a giant in my eyes.

The following year a woman named Kitty from the National Rifle Association contacted me saying one of the highest awards in the National Rifle Association had been bestowed upon me, the Leather Stocking Award. This award was given to me in the archery category. I dedicated the award to Jerry Boren, for without him, I would not have had this adventure of a lifetime.

SWEET AND SOUR LION

MARINADE INGREDIENTS:

1 tsp soy sauce
Rice wine to cover meat

1-2 tsp of corn starch

MEAT INGREDIENTS

1/2 pound Mountain Lion
   tenderloin, cut into bite-
   sized pieces
1 small can pineapple bits

1/2 each yellow, red and
   green bell pepper
1 clove garlic, minced
Oil for frying

BATTER INGREDIENTS:

1/2 cup water
2 T flour
1 T corn starch

1/2 tsp baking soda
1 egg
1 tsp oil

SAUCE INGREDIENTS:

1-1/2 T ketchup
1 tsp plum sauce
1/4 tsp Worcestershire
    sauce

1 tsp oyster sauce
1 tsp cornstarch
1 tsp sugar

INSTRUCTIONS

Mix meat with marinated and refrigerate 1 hour to overnight.

Remove meat from marinade and pat dry.

Mix batter, coat meat and fry in a large skillet or wok at medium-high heat. Set aside and drain most of the oil from the pan.

Brown garlic, then add peppers and pineapple and sauté for 5 minutes.

Mix sauce ingredients and add to pan. Heat until thickened.

Serve over steamed rice.

COLORADO MULE DEER

After much research, I decided I wanted my Mule Deer challenge to take place in Colorado. The only problem was, I had to wait three years before I was finally selected by the state's draw system. I harvested this animal employing a Texas hotshot, and the result was well worth the wait because this was a Boone and Crockett record book-level animal that had a green score of 204, with a 197 after the 60-day drying period.

SWEET MULE DEER SAUSAGE

INGREDIENTS

10 lbs mule deer trimmings
1 lb side bacon
Montreal Steak Seasoning
Cumin seed
HY's Seasoning Salt
    without MSG or our
    favorite seasoned salt

3 lb pork loin
3/4 cup chopped garlic
1-1/2 cups processed honey
    (not the solid raw ver-
    sion)
Hot pepper flakes (optional)

INSTRUCTIONS

Grind the mule deer, bacon, and pork through a medium screen, alternating chunks of mule deer meat with bacon and pork. On a clean flat surface, flatten the ground meat to the thickness of a pizza crust, then season liberally with the spices. Next, spoon dollops of garlic onto the meat and pour the honey over it all. Mix very well with your hands, using a kneading motion, until the mixture is as homogeneous as possible.

Take a small portion of the sausage mixture, make it into a patty, fry it over medium-high heat, and then taste it to see if you need to adjust the seasonings. Continue to do this until the sausage has the flavor you want.

Once you've achieved the desired flavor, either put it through the stuffer to make cased sausages, or package it up like burgers for country style sausages.

MULE DEER SAUSAGE BREAD

INGREDIENTS

1 pound venison sausage

1 large package shredded mozzarella

2 eggs

1 package fresh pizza dough

1 T oregano

3 T onions, diced

2 T Parmesan cheese

3 T red and green peppers, diced

3 T canned mushroom pieces

Other pizza ingredients of your choice in small amounts

Marinara sauce (optional)

INSTRUCTIONS

Preheat oven to 350° F.

Remove Sweet Deer Mule sausage from casing. Brown sausage in iron skillet, drain and let cool slightly.

Whisk 2 egg whites and one egg yolk together, reserving the remaining yolk for later.

Add mozzarella, sausage, peppers, onions, mushrooms and oregano with egg mixture and stir to coat.

Press dough onto greased cookie sheet in a rectangular shape. Spoon sausage/egg/cheese mixture into middle of dough and bring long sides together in the middle and fold together. Crimp ends.

Place bread seam side down on greased baking sheet and brush the top with the remaining egg yolk and sprinkle Parmesan cheese over top.

Bake for 30 minutes or until crust is golden brown. Remove from oven and cool slightly before serving.

Great dipped in marinara sauce.

ARCTIC MUSKOX CHALLENGE

My search for the Arctic Muskox took me to the North Westt territories of Canada, where I booked Guided Arctic Expeditions to lead me on the hunt. This was a cold one, with temperatures on day three of –25° F! I stalked the Muskox with my bow and closed the deal on this award winner with my third arrow. Harvesting this muskox earned my second Leather Stocking Award from the National Rifle Association.

MUSKOX TENDERLOIN WITH CRANBERRY COULIS

INGREDIENTS

8-12 oz loin (remove from fridge about 30 minutes before cooking)
Maldon Sea Salt

1 T cracked Tellicherry peppercorns
1 T Olive Oil
1 T Butter

CRANBERRY COULIS

4 T fresh cranberries
2 oz light red wine

2 tsp orange juice, fresh squeezed

SIDE DISH INGREDIENTS

1 T butter
1/2 clove garlic, finely
   minced assorted fresh
   vegetables

1 medium potato, boiled
2 T lemon juice

INSTRUCTIONS

Preheat oven to 350°F.

Simmer the cranberries in the orange juice until they just start to burst. Set aside and keep warm.

Place peppercorns in a cloth to cover, then lightly crack them with the flat side of a meat tenderizing mallet.

Dry off the loin with paper towels and top with cracked peppercorns and sea salt.

Add olive oil and butter to cast iron skillet, melt and stir to combine well.

Sear peppercorn side of meat for 3-4 minutes for medium rare. Flip the meat and cook an additional 3 minutes. Remove to a warmed plate an cover with aluminum foil to rest.

Turn down the heat and deglaze the pan with wine, then add cranberry mixture and stir to heat.

Slice Muskox and pour cranberry mixture over meat.

Serve with fresh vegetables sautéed in garlic butter and sprinkled with lemon juice.

MUSKOX BARLEY SOUP

INGREDIENTS

2 lbs Muskox meat

2 large onions, chopped

2 celery stalks, chopped

1 carrot, sliced thin

1/2 small zucchini, sliced

1 garlic clove

1 T butter

1/4 cup sherry

2 tsp dried basil or 2 T fresh

3-4 crushed peppercorns

2 potatoes diced very small

1/2 cup barley

1 sprig rosemary

1 bay leaf

INSTRUCTIONS

Cut meat into 1-inch cubes. Brown meat, onions and garlic clove in butter.

When meat is browned, fill pot with water and add seasonings. Simmer for an hour or until meat is tender. Add barley and simmer.

Just before barley is done, add potatoes and zucchini cook just until potatoes are fork-tender.

Remove bay leaf and rosemary sprig before serving.

Serve with fresh, crusty bread.

CANADIAN MOOSE — FINALLY!

After 10 years, I finally got a moose tag for the state of Maine because my good friend, Jeff, transferred his tag to me. So, in late August I set out with another friend, Joe Ferraro, to fulfill my moose harvesting dream. The moose led us on a tough hunt, but the wait and the effort was worth it for this amazing 900+ pound animal.

Jeff, my guide, and I pose with my 40-inch Canadian moose.

MOOSE SIRLOIN STEAK
WITH SAUTÉED MUSHROOMS AND RED WINE SAUCE

INGREDIENTS

4 7-ounce Moose sirloin
　　steaks, room temperature
2 T plus 1 tsp olive oil
Kosher salt, to taste
Fresh ground pepper, to taste
2 T shallot, minced
1 cup red wine

1/2 tsp pepper, coarsely
　　ground
1 cup beef stock (homemade
　　or packaged)
6 T unsalted butter
10 oz mushrooms of your
　　choice, sliced

INSTRUCTIONS

Pat the steaks dry with paper towels and massage them with 2 T of olive oil. Liberally season both sides of the steaks with Kosher salt and freshly ground pepper:

Melt 1 T butter in a small saucepan over medium heat. Add the minced shallot, and sauté for 3 to 4 minutes until just starting to caramelize. Stir in the wine and pepper, and bring to a low boil. Let it reduced to 1/2 cup, about 10 minutes. Stir in the beef stock and bring it to a low boil, letting it reduce half again, about 10 more minutes. The sauce should now be shiny with a deep rich brown color. Remove from heat. (You can prepare the sauce ahead of time and re-warm it.)

Preheat oven to 450° F. Melt 1 T of butter in a heavy skillet over medium heat. When the foam subsides, add the sliced mushrooms. Sprinkle them with salt and pepper, and cook until golden brown. Transfer to a plate with slotted spoon.

Heat 2 T butter and 1 tsp of olive oil in the same skillet over medium-high heat. When the foam subsides, add the Moose steaks and brown both sides, 2 minutes per side.

Transfer the skillet to the preheated oven, and roast the steaks 8 to 10 minutes, depending on the thickness, to medium-rare. (Take care to not over-cook, as the meat dries out easily.)

Take the skillet out of the oven and pour the cooking juices from the steaks into the sauce. Rewarm the sauce over low heat and whisk in the 2 remaining T butter, one-half T at a time, until the sauce takes on a satiny sheen.

To serve, scatter some mushrooms over each moose steak, and drizzle the sauce on top and around each steak.

SPIRITED MOOSE MEATBALLS

INGREDIENTS

2 lbs moose, ground

1/4 cup Worcestershire sauce

1-1/4 cups fresh bread crumbs, fine

1 tsp salt

1 egg, beaten

1 tsp pepper

1 T parsley

3 T butter

1 onion, finely diced

1/3 cup good quality bourbon whiskey

2 cups of your favorite BBQ sauce

MEATBALL INSTRUCTIONS

Preheat oven to 450° F.

Add ground moose to mixing bowl and break up.

Add egg, Worcestershire sauce, bread crumbs, parsley, salt and pepper and gently mix this together with your hands until just combined.

Make rounded T size meatballs with your hands and place on large baking sheet. Bake 20 minutes.

SAUCE INSTRUCTIONS

Sauté the onions in butter until golden brown. Pour in bourbon and simmer for 1-2 minutes. Stir in BBQ sauce and heat through.

Place baked meatballs in a small Crockpot® and pour sauce over the top. Gently stir to coat. Cover and cook on low for 30 minutes.

TEXAS AOUDAD

I traveled to Texas to hunt Aoudad Sheep with my friends, Joe and Steve. Using a rock outcropping, I waited for the sheep to move into position and took my shot. He was the sixth sheep in my collection, and had great bases and a beautiful set of horns.

SLOW-COOKED AOUDAD SHEEP CURRY

INGREDIENTS

1 Aoudad backstrap, cubed
   in large chunks
6-8 T curry powder
1 T allspice
2 onions, chopped)
1 ginger root
6-7 cloves garlic

1 jalapeño pepper, chopped
1 can coconut milk
1 can diced tomatoes
1 tsp thyme
1 tsp cayenne pepper
1 tsp garlic powder
Vegetable oil

INSTRUCTIONS

Mix garlic powder, cayenne pepper, and 1 T curry and sprinkle cubed meat. Cook diced onions and ginger slightly and then add meat and lightly brown. Remove the meat and let it rest in a bowl.

Dice 1 onion, ginger, and 4-6 cloves of garlic. Place in blender or food processor and blend until the mixture is smooth.

Place Aoudad meat, blended mixture, diced tomatoes, coconut milk, jalapeño and two cups of water in slow cooker. Add thyme, allspice, and remaining curry and stir together. Cook on low for 6-8 hours, or until meat is fork-tender.

Serve with mashed potatoes, rice or roasted root vegetables.

DALL SHEEP STARTS MY GRAND SLAM

Hunting the Dall Sheep was a physically challenging proposition. My choice for an outfitter for this trip to the Copper River in Alaska was easy — Mel Gillis, a good friend and renowned sheep hunter. This record Dall Sheep rolled 800 yards down a mountainside. I carried the head and hide in my backpack and follow a drainage basin back to camp. It took more than 17 hours to complete this hunt, and I ended up with 16 blisters on my feet. It was rough, but well worth it to fill the first leg of my grand slam.

DALL SHEEP CHILI

INGREDIENTS

2 lbs Dall Sheep meat, finely
    ground
2 cups chili beans
1 can chopped tomatoes
1 can tomato sauce
1 cup water
1/2 cup black olives, chopped
Salt to taste

1 to 1-1/2 tsp red pepper
1 to 1-1/2 tsp black pepper
Chili powder to taste
Chopped onions and
    shredded cheese
    jalapeño, avocado, etc.
    for garnish,

INSTRUCTIONS

Pour all the ground sheep meat into a thick walled cooking pot, stir well and cook until browned. Drain grease and discard. Put meat back into pot, then add all ingredients except chopped onions and grated cheese.

Put lid on pot and reduce to a simmer. Cook for 4 hours.

Garnish with chopped onions, jalapeños and grated cheese.

A good accompaniment for this chili is corn bread.

It's always a good idea to have a plan. Sheep have sharp eyesight and they can pick up movement from long distances so a plan that implements stealth is required.

STONE SHEEP IS #2 IN MY GRAND SLAM

I set my sights on British Columbia and Scope Lake Outfitters for this hunt. My son and my good friend Jimmy traveled to the Yukon with me for this hunt. Using my trusty Winchester 7mm, I harvested a beautiful full-curl sheep and bagged the second animal in my quest for a grand slam.

OVEN BRAISED STONE SHEEP SHANKS

INGREDIENTS

3 T olive oil, divided
1 T butter
1 large onion, coarsely
    chopped
1 rib of celery, coarsely
    chopped
1 medium carrot, coarsely
    chopped
4 cloves garlic, sliced
4 stone sheep shanks

1 dash salt and freshly
    ground black pepper
1 cup dry red wine
3 T tomato paste
2 cups chicken broth
1 cup beef broth
1/4 cup cider vinegar
4 sprigs fresh thyme
1 bay leaf

INSTRUCTIONS

Heat the oven to 325° F.

In a large skillet or Dutch oven, heat 1 T of olive oil with butter. Add chopped onion, celery, and carrot. Cook, stirring until onion is softened. Add garlic and cook, stirring, for 2 minutes more. Remove to a large roasting pan, or Dutch oven.

Add rest of olive oil skillet. Sprinkle the sheep shanks with salt and pepper; saute over medium heat for about 8 minutes, turning to sear all sides. Add to chopped vegetables.

Deglaze skillet with the red wine. Simmer for 2 minutes. Add tomato paste, chicken broth, beef broth, and vinegar. Bring to a boil. Reduce heat and simmer 5 minutes. Pour over sheep shanks and add fresh thyme and bay leaf.

Cover pan tightly and bake for 1-1/2 hours. Remove lid and continue baking for 2 to 2-1/2 hours, turning the shanks occasionally. Meat should be very tender when done.

ROSEMARY IRISH STONE SHEEP

INGREDIENTS

1 T olive oil
1 large onion, chopped
1-1/2 lbs sheep shoulder
1/2 tsp salt
1/2 tsp pepper
1 can beef broth
2 cups water

1/2 tsp dried thyme
3 sprigs rosemary
2 carrots, large slices
4-5 small red potatoes, halved
5-6 small tomatoes (optional)

INSTRUCTIONS

Pre-heat oven to 375° F.

Heat oil in a skillet over medium high heat, sauté onions until golden, then place in a 2-1/2 quart baking dish.

Salt and pepper sheep, and in the same skillet brown both sides of the meat, then put on top of onions in dish.

Pour beef broth and water over meat and onions, add seasonings, cover with tin foil and braise for 1 hour. Remove foil and continue to braise for another hour.

Serve with juices from dish.

END OF A 14-YEAR WAIT FOR BIGHORN

I'd been applying for a draw for a big horn sheep in Wyoming for 14 years, and finally got one. I was headed to Casper with the outfitter for this hunt, Fritz Meyer. I managed to harvest the third sheep in my grand slam, even though I was ill. After two days of recovery, my harvest was recorded and plugged.

GRILLED BIGHORN BACKSTRAP

INGREDIENTS

1 Bighorn backstrap loin, approximately 12 inches long
2 cloves garlic, minced

3 T butter
Dash lemon pepper
Dash of rubbed sage
1/2 cup butter, melted

INSTRUCTIONS

Clean backstrap thoroughly, and trim all excess fat and muscle sheath. Rub lemon pepper and sage on backstrap and place in 13 x 9-inch dish.

Brown minced garlic in 1 T of butter in skillet over low heat, then pour over backstrap.

Cover and refrigerate for several hours so meat absorbs seasonings.

Sear both sides of backstrap quickly on very hot grill or skillet to seal in juices, then brush on melted butter and cook to taste on cooler place on grill. Turn several times and baste often.

Meat should be served medium to rare. (The longer you cook, the dryer and tougher the meat will be).

Note: Cutting into steaks will allow for faster grilling, but be cautious about over-seasoning and overcooking. Bighorn sheep meat has a delicate flavor and can easily be overpowered by heavy seasoning.

COORS BIGHORN SHEEP STEW

INGREDIENTS

Vegetable oil
2 lbs bighorn sheep, cut into
 1-1/2 inch cubes
Flour for dredging
2 cloves garlic, minced
1 6-oz can tomato paste
2-1/4 cups Coors beer
2 bay leaves
1 tsp salt
1 tsp beef bouillon granules
1 tsp sugar
1/2 lb mushrooms, halved

1-1/2 tsp freshly ground
 black pepper
1/2 tsp dried thyme
3/4 tsp dried oregano
8 to 10 pearl onions, peeled
6 carrots, peeled and cut into
 chunks
6 stalks celery, cut into
 chunks
6 small potatoes, peeled and
 cut into chunks

INSTRUCTIONS

Heat 1/4 inch of oil in large skillet until shimmering. Dredge meat in flour and brown in hot oil. Transfer to large kettle.

Add remaining ingredients. Cook over low heat for 3 hours or until meat is tender.

Serves 6

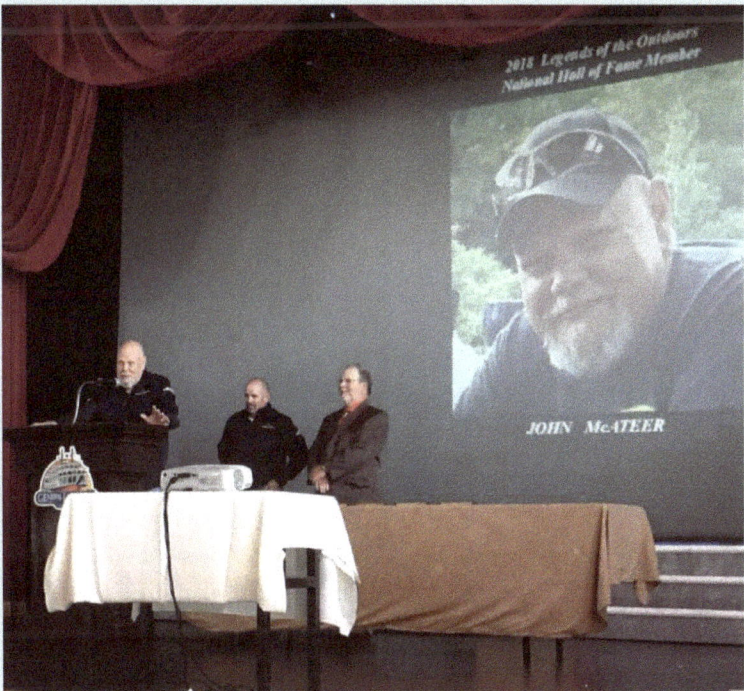

John's 2018 Induction into the Legends of Outdoors National Hall of Fame.

GRAND SLAM COMPLETE!

The wait for this hunt had been ten long years. Finally, my friend Johnny Zenz told me Nevada planned to have an auction for a Governor's License, which I won! We headed to Reno, Nevada to harvest the Desert Bighorn sheep that would complete my North American Wild Sheep Grand Slam.

JUNIPERBERRY RUBBED DESERT BIGHORN BACKSTRAPS

INGREDIENTS

1-2 lbs strips of boneless
   Bighorn Loin (properly
   dry aged at least 2 weeks)
3-4 T olive oil

2 T fresh garlic, minced
3-4 T rub (see below)
Kosher or Sea Salt to taste

RUB INGREDIENTS

2 tsp juniper berries
1 tsp black peppercorns
1/2 tsp kosher salt
1/2 tsp crushed red pepper

1 bay leaf
2 T extra-virgin olive oil
6 sage leaves, minced
1 garlic clove, minced

INSTRUCTIONS

Trim all the silver skin from the loin. Brush with olive oil, and rub the meat with the garlic, then massage the meat with the rub. For the best results place in a zip lock bag overnight to allow the seasonings to penetrate.

Cook either over a very hot grill OR quick sear in an iron skillet. Quickly sear and cook evenly on all sides until rare (125° F internal temperature).

Allow the meat to rest to redistribute the moisture and let the residual heat finish the meat to a juicy medium rare.

THIS IS TO CERTIFY THAT

John McAteer

has documented with

GSC OVIS

the successful taking of the four species of North American wild sheep, and has been

1046

in recognition of the

Grand Slam

YEAR COMPLETED

2002

Dennis

GSCO Executi

BATTLING HIGH ALTITUDES FOR A TIBETAN BLUE SHEEP

I traveled all the way to the mountains of Tibet for this high altitude hunt. It was cold and the air was thin, but we kept climbing until I saw my ram using a 7mm mag with a 160-grain Nosler Partition Bullet. This was sheep number six for me.

High in the mountains with my Tibetan Blue sheep.

TIBETAN BLUE SHEEP AND RICE PILAF

INGREDIENTS

2 cups basmati rice

4 heads garlic, whole

1/2 cup vegetable oil

2 lbs boneless leg of sheep, cut into 3-inch pieces

2 large onions, thinly sliced

2 T cumin seed

2 T coriander seed

1/2 cup fresh barberries or chopped sour cherries

1 tsp whole black peppercorns

2 cups boiling water to cover

2 T salt

INSTRUCTIONS

Place basmati rice in a large bowl and cover with warm water. Set aside. Wash heads of garlic. Set aside.

Heat oil in a dutch oven or large skillet over high heat until smoking, then add meat, turning occasionally until it is evenly browned, about 10 minutes. Stir in the onions; cook and stir until the onion has softened and browned, about 10 minutes.

Stir in the carrots; cook and stir until they have softened, about 10 minutes. Sprinkle with cumin, coriander, barberries/cherries, and peppercorns. Drop whole garlic heads into the mixture, stirring to distribute ingredients.

Reduce heat to medium. Cover and cook for 30 minutes.

Drain rice then wash with hot water. Pour cleaned rice over the sheep mixture in an even layer. Slowly pour in the boiling water. The rice should be covered with about 3/4 inch of water. Do not stir. Season with salt, and reduce heat to medium-low. Cover and cook until rice is tender, about 20 minutes. Stir rice and lamb together, and serve with the garlic heads on top.

GREAT TURKEY IN SC

Below I'm pictured with a turkey that I harvested in South Carolina. It was a great bird with an 11-inch beard and inch and a quarter spurs.

MOIST ROASTED WILD TURKEY

INGREDIENTS

10-12 lb whole turkey

2 sticks butter, cut into tablespoons

3 large carrots, cut into large chunks

table salt

3 medium sweet onions, quartered

3 medium tart/sweet apple, halved with seeds removed

3 stalks celery, cut into large chunks

1/4 cup dried summer savory

INSTRUCTIONS

Use electric roaster oven (preferred) or large, heavy pot with a tight-fitting lid.

Wash turkey inside and out and pat dry. Place in roaster or pot, breast side up.

Rub salt liberally inside body cavity and add 1 T of summer savory so that it coats most of the cavity. Add apple quarters, and two chunks each of carrot, celery and onion (or equal number that will fit inside)

Use your fingers to separate skin from breast meat, then slide 4 T of butter under skin on each side. Pull skin back down to cover breast meat

Rub the outside of the bird liberally with salt, then sprinkle the remaining summer savory over bird. Cover breasts with heavy duty aluminum foil to prevent them from cooking too quickly.

Place remaining vegetables, apples and butter around bird and fill roaster/pot with water until it is about 2 inches deep.

Cook at 325° F for 2 hours, then check dark meat temperature. Bird is done when interior dark meat temperature reaches 150°-155° F. When meat is done, turn off heat and allow meat to steam for 30 minutes.

Carve meat and submerge in broth left in roaster/pot for an additional 30 minutes. Use broth to make gravy if desired.

BERCHELL'S ZEBRA

Day two of my African hunting trip I stumbled upon a herd of Berchell's zebras. After two hours, I spotted a beautiful stallion who'd led a rough life. Using my Winchester 375 H&H safari rifle , my 300-grain bullet found its mark, and I had a beautiful zebra. My first African animal was in the books.

BRAISED ZEBRA

INGREDIENTS

2 lbs zebra meat, cut into chunks

1 lb tomatoes, peeled seeded and chopped

2 onions, chopped

2 T flour

1 tsp paprika

1/4 cup olive oil

Pinches salt, pepper, turmeric, coriander, cayenne

1 cup browned bone stock

1/4 cup heavy cream

1 bay leaf

A good jigger of sherry

INSTRUCTIONS

Fry the onion golden in the oil and remove to a plate.

Dust the meat with flour, salt, and pepper, and brown in oil.

Add tomatoes and onions to the pan, stir briefly to take up the crusty bits on the bottom of the pan, then add the sherry, stock, and spices.

Simmer until tender, which may take a while if the beast was old. Before serving, whisk in the heavy cream.

My friend Joseph Ferraro also harvested a zebra.

ZEBRA STEW

INGREDIENTS

2 lbs of zebra, cut into chunks

2 onions, chopped

2 tomatoes, peeled, seeded, and chopped

2 green plantains, peeled and cut into chunks

2 sweet potatoes, and cut into chunks

2 or 3 chilies, minced

1 T ginger, minced

2 large regular potatoes, cubed

1 can (1-1/2 cups) coconut milk (santen)

1 or 2 cups browned bone stock

1 clove garlic, minced

Salt, pepper, pinches of ground clove and nutmeg to taste

INSTRUCTIONS

Rub the garlic, ginger, chilies, salt, and pepper into the meat, and let it rest for one or two hours in the refrigerator.

Then brown it in a heavy casserole with a little oil. When it is well seared, add the stock and spices and simmer for an hour.

Then add the vegetables and scant water to cover. Simmer until the vegetables are tender.

Mix in the coconut milk before serving.

WILD WILDEBEEST ADVENTURE

This hunt involved the blue wildebeest, also known as the poor man's buffalo. It had been injured by a pack of wild dogs and I'd been asked to dispatch it. These animals have a tendency to charge when injured, so this was a pretty dangerous undertaking. The animal was indeed injured, and it charged my PH and was only 20 yards from him when I hit the mark and took it down. This adventure was truly an adrenaline rush!

ROAST BEEST LEG

YOGURT MARINADE

This recipe is for a large leg of wildebeest.

Marinate meat overnight in a plastic bag using enough plain yogurt to cover.

Next day, rinse the yogurt off, dry the piece of meat and rub it well with the following mixture:

RUB INGREDIENTS

1/2 cup brown sugar

1/2 cup paprika

1 T ground black pepper

1 T salt

1 T chili powder

1 T garlic powder

1 T onion powder

ROASTING INGREDIENTS

7 cloves garlic, crushed   Water

apple cider vinegar

INSTRUCTIONS

Add garlic, 2 cups water mixed with a two Ts of vinegar to a large roasting pan.

Add meat and roast in a slow oven, 330°F (170°C).

Add water and vinegar mixture as needed to keep moist throughout roasting process.

Cooking time will be according to size, for large leg: about around 2 hours or more.

WILDEBEEST SIRLOIN

INGREDIENTS

1/2 tsp salt

1 lb wildebeest sirloin, sinew removed

2 cups good-quality dry red wine

1 T black peppercorns

2 T fresh ginger, chopped

2 T cinnamon

1/2 tsp grated nutmeg

1 pinch saffron

2 T brown sugar

1 cup water

1 T butter

1 T olive oil

INSTRUCTIONS

Rub the salt into the meat and refrigerate for 1 hour.

Place the remaining ingredients in a saucepan and bring to boil. Leave to cool.

Once cool, pour the marinade over the meat and refrigerate overnight.

The following day, remove the meat and pat dry.

Reserve the marinade.

Preheat the oven to 425°F (220° C).

Heat olive oil in a frying pan and add butter and melt.

Add the meat and brown well.

Place the meat in the oven and cook to desired stage: 3-4 minutes for medium-rare.

Heat reserved marinade and use as sauce for sirloin.

A QUICK GEMSBOK HUNT

I started this day looking for Cape Buffalo, but found this nice Gemsbok instead. I took my Browning 7 mm and managed to work my way to within 100 yards of my prey. With one well-placed shot, I had just taken my second great trophy on this amazing hunt in Africa. Boy, was I proud of it!

GEMSBOK STIR-FRY

2 T Shaoxing wine or dry sherry

1/2 tsp salt

3 T soy sauce

1 T potato or corn starch mixed with 2 T water

STIR-FRY INGREDIENTS

1 lb gemsbok, trimmed of fat

1-1/2 cups peanut or other cooking oil

1 to 4 fresh red chilies

3 garlic cloves, slivered

1 T soy sauce

1/2 red and 1/2 yellow bell pepper, sliced

1 bunch cilantro, roughly chopped

2 tsp sesame oil

vegetables of your choice

sesame seeds for garnish

INSTRUCTIONS

Stir marinade ingredients together in large bowl or add to plastic bag large enough to hold meat.

Slice the meat into thin slivers — 1-3 inches long and about 1/4 inch wide. Mix with the marinade and set aside while you cut all the other ingredients and prepare rice for cooker or stove-top cooking. Time this so that it will be finished cooking by the time your stir-fry is ready.

Heat the peanut oil in a wok or large heavy pot until it reaches 275°F to 290°F. Don't let it get too hot. Add about 1/3 of the meat to the hot oil and use a chopstick or butter knife to separate the meat slices the second they hit the hot oil. Let them sizzle for 30 seconds to 1 minute. Remove with a spider skimmer or slotted spoon. Set aside and cook the remaining meat one-third at a time.

Pour out all but about 3 T of the oil.

Place the pan with the remaining hot oil over high heat. The moment it begins to smoke, add the chilies and bell peppers and stir-fry for 90 seconds. Next, add the garlic and cook another 30 seconds, then add the cooked meat and stir fry another 90 seconds.

Add the cilantro and soy sauce, then stir fry a final 30 seconds, or just until the cilantro wilts. Turn off the heat and stir in the sesame oil.

Serve at once with steamed rice.

GEMSBOK FRICASSEE

INGREDIENTS

1/2 lb gemsbok fillet, sliced

olive oil

3 T butter

1/2 onion, thinly sliced

1 clove garlic, crushed

1 cup mixed mushrooms
  such as shiitake,
  Portobelo, bellini, etc.

1 cup shredded cabbage

1 cup good beef stock

1/2 cup cream

1 cup port

sprigs of rosemary

olive oil

salt and freshly ground
  pepper

INSTRUCTIONS

To make the fricassee, heat a little olive oil and a T of butter in a pan. Add the onion and slowly cook until it's slightly caramelized.

Turn up the heat and add the garlic and the mushrooms, along with another T of butter. Cook on high heat until the mushrooms are just tender, then add the cabbage and cook for 1 minute.

Finish with a T of beef stock and the cream. Leave to simmer until the cream has reduced. Season to taste.

Next, heat a heavy frying pan to smoking. Add a dash of olive oil and a T of butter. Sear the meat well, then lower the heat and leave to cook to desired doneness. Remove from pan and let rest.

Deglaze the pan with port, add the fricassee and a sprig of rosemary and let it reduce until thickened. Sir in meat and serve.

STALKING GREATER KUDU

O n the fifth day of my African odyssey, we headed to the vast plains to stalk greater kudu. After hiding behind a five-foot ant hill, I saw my target. At a range of 347 yards, the kudu was in the sites of my 7 MM. Using 150-grain bullets, I too my shot.

KALAHARI SALTED KUDU WITH SWEET POTATOES

INGREDIENTS

2-3 T coarse sea salt

1 T freshly crushed garlic

3 T fresh chopped herbs (rosemary, thyme, oregano)

2 T freshly ground black pepper

3 T olive oil

1 whole kudu fillet (approximately 4 lbs), cubed

1 lb Japanese white sweet potatoes, cut into 1/2-inch thick slices*

Sea Salt for sprinkling on potatoes

INSTRUCTIONS FOR KUDU

Mix the Sea Salt (coarse), crushed garlic, fresh herbs, black pepper and olive oil.

Roll the fillet in this mixture, rubbing it onto the meat so that it sticks.

Braise over hot to medium coals. Turn the fillet until it is cooked to your liking. If oven roasting, sear the fillet first by browning on each side in a large frying pan. Finish off in a hot oven at 400°F for about 20-35 minutes depending on how well done you would like it.

Rest for a few minutes before slicing into thick medallions. Season to taste.

INSTRUCTIONS FOR SWEET POTATOES

Arrange sweet potato slices in a baking dish. Drizzle with olive oil and roast them at 350°F for about 30 minutes, or until they are golden and crisp. Sprinkle with coarse sea salt and serve with the fillet.

* Substitute yams or orange sweet potatoes if you cannot find the Japanese variety.

MARINATED GRILLED KUDU KABOBS

INGREDIENTS

Kudu loin cut into 2-inch pieces

1/2 cup coriander leaves

1/2 cup sweet basil

1/3 cup lemon juice

1/2 cup olive oil

1/2 cup Italian flat leaf parsley

2 T dark soy sauce

5 cloves garlic, crushed

vegetables of choice, cubed (onions, peppers, etc.

INSTRUCTIONS

Mix all ingredients together in plastic bag, then add meat and let it marinate overnight in fridge.

Alternate meat and vegetables on kabob skewers and grill over very hot coals for 2–3 minutes on each side for medium rare meat.

TINY DUIKER IN RUGGED TERRAIN

T he hunt this day moved us to a more rugged location near a watering hole, where we noticed some common Duiker. These are tiny animals, who run zigzag maneuvers to escape danger. We managed to get within 85 yards and at that point I closed the deal with my 7mm. Suddenly, I had another beautiful specimen

DUIKER GOULASH

INGREDIENTS

1 pound ground Duiker

1/4 cup chopped green bell pepper

1/4 cup chopped onion

2 T chopped fresh chives

15 1/4 ounces whole kernel corn, drained

2 red potatoes (cubed)

1 stalk celery (thinly sliced)

1 tomato (chopped)

42 ounces beef broth

1 cup water

1 cup elbow macaroni

salt

black pepper

1/4 tsp garlic powder (or to taste)

INSTRUCTIONS

Stir the Duiker, bell pepper, onion, and chives together in a large pot over medium heat until the vegetables are very tender and the Duiker has browned, about 10 minutes.

Stir in the corn, red potatoes, celery, tomato, beef broth, water, and macaroni. Bring to a boil over high heat; reduce heat to medium-low, cover, and simmer until the potatoes are tender — about 30 minutes more.

Season to taste with salt, pepper, and garlic powder before serving.

GRILLED BACON-WRAPPED DUIKER

INGREDIENTS

1 Duiker loin, cut into steaks

bacon, enough to wrap each steak

3/4 cup dry red wine

1/4 cup soy sauce

2 tsp dry mustard

1 T honey

steak seasoning (see recipe on following page)

1 T fresh thyme

1 T fresh rosemary

2 tsp. Worcestershire sauce

1 T brown sugar

TENDERLOIN SEASONING

2 T crushed black pepper

2 T garlic powder

2 T kosher salt

2 T paprika

1 T onion powder

1 T ground coriander

1 T dried dill

1 T crushed red pepper flakes

INSTRUCTIONS

In a glass measuring cup mix the wine, soy sauce, dry mustard powder, Worcestershire sauce, honey and brown sugar. Place the steaks in a heavy-duty zip-lock bag and pour marinade in. Place in a dish and set in refrigerator for 1-2 hours.

Prepare charcoal grill for indirect heat. Light the grill and wait until it reaches medium heat (350° F).

Remove steaks from marinade and blot with paper towels. Sprinkle liberally with the steak seasoning, fresh thyme and rosemary. Wrap meat with bacon.

Cook over medium heat until the internal temperature reaches 135° F. Cover and rest 5 minutes before serving.

EASY DAY HUNTING BLESBOK

This day was dedicated to looking for a nice Blesbok. We sited about 20 Blesbok and this was going to be an easy stalk because we had good cover. I took an off-shoulder 200-yard shot using my 7mm mag and was able to harvest a beautiful Blonde Blesbok.

BLESBOK CURRY

INGREDIENTS

2-1/2 inch fresh ginger, peeled and chopped

5 garlic cloves, peeled and chopped

2-3 fresh green chilies, chopped

1 T whole coriander seeds

1/4 cup olive oil

2 medium onions, thinly sliced

1/4 tsp ground turmeric

1 carrot, sliced

2 lbs Blesbok backstrap, cut into 1-1/2 inch cubes

1 tsp cayenne pepper

3 14-oz cans whole tomatoes

1 tsp salt and freshly ground black pepper

2 whole cardamom pods

1 cinnamon stick

4 potatoes, cut into chunks

1/2 tsp garam masala (see recipe below)

GARAM MASALA

1 T cumin

2 tsp coriander

2 tsp cardamon

1-1/2 tsp cinnamon

1 tsp pepper

1/2 tsp nutmeg

1/2 tsp cloves

1/2 tsp cayenne

INSTRUCTIONS

Finely chop the ginger, garlic and green chilies. Grind the coriander seeds to a coarse powder in a coffee or spice grinder and set aside.

Heat the oil in a large, heavy saucepan over medium-high heat. Add the onions and cook until golden brown, stirring often, about 5 minutes. Stir in the ginger mixture and cook for 2 minutes.

Add the meat and cook for 1-2 additional minutes, then add the turmeric, cayenne pepper and ground coriander, coating the meat well.

Add the tomatoes and seasoning and stir, then cover and cook on medium-high heat for 10 minutes.

Add the cardamom and cinnamon, and cook for a further 10 minutes.

Add the potatoes, stir, cover and reduce heat to low. Simmer for at least one hour or until the meat is tender.

Sprinkle the garam masala over the curry and rest for at least 15 minutes before serving.

Serve with steamed basmati rice, poppadoms (flatbread), mint yogurt and a tomato/chili sauce. Scatter with fresh coriander just before serving.

BACON WRAPPED BLESBOK

INGREDIENTS

1-2 lbs blesbok roast, cut into large chunks

3.5 oz plain yogurt

1 cup bacon bits

1 lb bacon

1 large onion, sliced thin

jar apricot jam

INSTRUCTIONS

Put Blesbok meat into large plastic bag and pour yogurt over to coat. Leave Blesbok in the yogurt overnight.

Next morning, preheat oven to 350°F.

Remove meat from yogurt and pat dry.

Mix bacon bits with apricot jam and spread onto top of each meat piece, then add onion slices.

Wrap each piece in bacon strips to cover completely and brush more jam mixture over bacon. Reserve remaining jam.

Place onions in baking disk and add meat.

Cover with foil and bake in oven at 350°F for 1-1/2 hours. Remove foil and bake an additional 15 minutes, or until bacon is crisp and glaze has carmelized. Use reserved jam as dipping sauce.

IMPRESSIVE IMPALA

We pointed our safari truck into the sun and headed west to a water hole for this hunt. Before we even reached our destination, we saw a small herd. My PH immediately handed me my 7mm mag and I was confident this was the right choice. I squeezed the trigger, and the Impala was down. I'd made yet another deposit in my memory bank.

SOUTH AFRICAN IMPALA CAMPFIRE POTJIE POT

INGREDIENTS

3-1/2 T sunflower oil

1/4 lb bacon, cut into cubes (optional)

1 medium) onion, peeled and roughly diced

2-4 lbs boneless impala meat, cut into cubes

2 medium carrot (about 1/3 cup), peeled and roughly diced

2 tsp sugar

1/2 lb whole baby potatoes

4-6 ears of corn on the cobs, cut into chunks

1 tsp dried sweet oregano

2 fresh/dried bay leaves

1 tsp salt

1/2 tsp freshly ground black pepper

1/2 lb dried apricots

1/2 cup good-quality South African dry red wine

4 cups beef/chicken stock

INSTRUCTIONS

Heat half of the sunflower oil in a medium traditional potjie pot (a cast iron, lidded pot with feet, as shown in photo on the previous page) on a hot fire. Sauté the bacon, if desired, until crispy. Add the onions and continue to sauté until the onions are golden brown Remove the bacon and onions from the pot and set aside.

Add the remaining sunflower oil and brown the impala cubes. Remove from pot and set aside.

Add the carrots and sugar to the pot and sauté until the sugar has melted and the carrots are caramelized.

Begin layering your potjie pot with the ingredients, starting with the impala cubes, bacon and onion mixture, carrots, baby potatoes, corn chunks, spices, salt and pepper and apricots. Add the red wine and stock and leave to cook for about 4 hours.

Serve with traditional African ipapa (grits), samp (similar to hominy), Mielie Meal (similar to polenta) or rice.

IMPALA CASSEROLE

INGREDIENTS

2 T olive oil

2-1/4 lbs impala meat cut into bite-sized pieces

1 medium potato, peeled and cubed

1 medium onion, chopped

2 medium parsnips, peeled and cubed

2 medium turnips, peeled and cubed

2 cups prepared beef stock

1/2 cup carrots, peeled and sliced

1/2 cup leeks, sliced

2-1/2 T garlic, crushed

1 bay leaf

1/2 cups red wine

1 can whole peeled tomatoes

1/8 tsp ground cumin

INSTRUCTIONS

Heat the oil in a large saucepan over a high heat. Once it is hot, add the meat and sauté until completely seared. Add the vegetables, garlic and bay leaf, and cook, stirring often, until browned.

Add the wine, reduce the heat and allow to simmer without the lid on until the wine has reduced. Add the tomatoes and then enough beef stock to cover the meat. Cover the saucepan and simmer for about 50 minutes until the meat is tender.

Add the cumin and season to taste with salt and pepper.

Serve hot with creamy mashed potatoes.

WARTHOG DREAM FULFILLED

Today we headed to the only watering hole in the area in search of a warthog. I'd been thinking about harvesting a warthog since the day I started talking about going to Africa. We approached the waterhole on foot and found a good vantage point where we could watch the wildlife come to drink. I saw my quarry, and he had a nice set of tusks. I decide to take a shot at him, and in an instant, I had my warthog. I was very happy hunter.

WARTHOG STEAK WITH CARAMELIZED APPLES

WARTHOG INGREDIENTS

3 T tomato sauce

2 T soy sauce

2 bay leaves

1 T chopped fresh sage

Splash of white wine

Kosher salt

1 T whole black peppercorns

Two 8-oz warthog fillets

Butter, for frying

1/4 cup barbecue sauce, for serving

CARAMELIZED APPLES

2 T golden syrup (you can substitute light corn syrup or honey or see recipe on next page)

1 T butter

1 T brown sugar

2 medium apples, unpeeled, cored and roughly chopped

1/4 cup barbecue sauce, for serving

INSTRUCTIONS

For the warthog: Put the tomato sauce, soy sauce, bay leaves, sage, black peppercorns and white wine in a bowl, add the warthog fillets and marinate at room temperature for 30 minutes.

Meanwhile, make the apples: Heat the golden syrup, butter and sugar together in a small frying pan until melted and starting to caramelize. Add the apples and toss to coat and soften a bit, about 3 minutes. Set aside.

To finish the warthog: Season the warthog fillets with salt. Heat a little butter in a frying pan and fry the warthog until just cooked through, 4 to 5 minutes on each side.

Serve immediately with the caramelized apples and some barbecue sauce.

GOLDEN SYRUP

INGREDIENTS

3 T water

1/2 cup sugar

1 lemon slice

2 1/2 cups sugar

1 1/4 cup boiling water

INSTRUCTIONS

Pour 3 T water and 1/2 cup sugar into a saucepan, and bring to a simmer over medium-low to medium heat.

While waiting for the mixture to cook, boil 1-1/4 cups water. Once the mixture turns a caramel color, slowly and carefully pour in the boiling water.

Add 2-1/2 cups sugar and bring to a low simmer, then add lemon slice. The lemon will keep the syrup from crystallizing as it simmers.

Turn the heat down to low and let the syrup simmer for about 45 minutes.

Remove the lemon slice and let syrup cool down for a few minutes before pouring it into a sterilized glass jar. The syrup will be thin at this point, but will thicken as it cools.

Store in a cool, dry place.

NOTE: *Nothing else tastes like this golden syrup, so it's worth the effort to make it and use for all sorts of things besides this recipe, including pancakes, waffles, French toast, scones, ice cream, fruit salad, and it can even be used in recipes as a substitute for honey.*

SOUTH AFRICAN WARTHOG BRAAI (BBQ)

The recommended method of cooking warthog according to this game recipe is over the coals of an open fire — better known as a braai in South Africa, or a BBQ in most other parts of the western world.

INGREDIENTS

1 large slab of warthog ribs

1-1/2 T cooking oil (sunflower is good)

4 large onions, peeled and sliced

1 small chili, seeded and finely chopped (if you like hot, spicy food, leave the seeds in)

2 T brown sugar

2 T curry powder (however mild or hot as you like)

1 tsp salt

1 tsp turmeric

2 T smooth apricot or peach jam

2 cups dry white wine

MARINADE INSTRUCTIONS

Heat the cooking oil in a pan on the stove and cook the chopped onion until it is soft and translucent. Add the chili and curry powder and cook gently while stirring. Add the rest of the ingredients, stir, and allow the mixture to simmer gently for about five minutes. Let marinade cool. Put the meat into a large dish or bag and pour the marinade over it. Put in refrigerator and leave overnight.

Your fire is ready if it's a mass of glowing coals with no flames showing. Remove meat from marinade and pat dry. Cook over fire on grid or on BBQ grill for 30 minutes, using the marinade to baste. Turn several times and continue basting until meat is cooked through.

LONG STEENBOK WAIT REWARDED

We were back at the same watering hole, and we used strategy when approaching it this time so we didn't spook the animals. We had a long wait on this day, but finally spotted a male steenbok. I didn't even think before I brought my rifle up and took the shot. All it took to get this trophy was a little patience.

STEENBOK SKEWERS

INGREDIENTS

Steenbok steaks cut into cubes

4 T hoisin sauce

1/4 cup soy sauce

1 T olive oil

1 T minced fresh ginger root

1/4 cup cilantro chopped

2 garlic cloves minced

1 white onion

1 red bell pepper, cubed

INSTRUCTIONS

Mix together hoisin sauce, soy sauce, garlic, olive oil, cilantro and ginger.

Cut steenbok steaks into cubes across grain on a diagonal. Place meat in a 1-gallon Ziploc® plastic bag. Pour hoisin sauce mixture over cubes, and mix well. Refrigerate 1 hour up to overnight.

Preheat an outdoor grill for high heat. Discard the marinade and thread steenbok pieces onto skewers with onion and pepper slices in between each piece.

Grill skewers 3 minutes per side, or to desired doneness.

Serve with a fresh salad and a side of hoisin sauce for extra dipping!

Tip: If you like things spicy, substitute red and green jalapeño peppers for the bell peppers.

STEENBOK MEATLOAF WITH BLOODY MARY KETCHUP

INGREDIENTS

1.5 lbs ground steenbok

1/2 cup panko or plain bread crumbs

1 egg, beaten

1 T yellow mustard

1 T Worcestershire sauce

1 T A-1 steak sauce

5 green chard leaves chopped (can substitute spinach)

1 yellow or green zucchini shaved into ribbons

1 garlic clove minced

2 T butter

BLOODY MARY KETCHUP

1 cup ketchup

Red pepper flakes to taste

2 T Bloody Mary seasoning (see recipe next page)

INSTRUCTIONS

Pre-heat oven to 400°F.

Heat skillet over medium heat. Add 2 T butter, garlic, chard and zucchini. Cook until soft and wilted. Remove from heat.

In a large bowl combine ground steenbok, panko, egg, mustard, Worcestershire sauce and A-1 and mix well. Add chard and zucchini and stir together.

Form meat into a loaf and place in a baking dish. Cover with foil and bake for 30 minutes.

Remove foil. Spoon Bloody Mary Ketchup on top of meatloaf and continue to cook for 10 minutes or until ketchup has slightly caramelized.

Serve with a side of smashed potatoes.

HOMEMADE BLOODY MARY SEASONING

INGREDIENTS

6 T grated horseradish

2 T Worcestershire sauce

6 big dashes of Tabasco®

1 tsp salt

1 tsp celery salt

1/2 tsp celery seed

1 ounce fresh lemon juice

1 ounce olive brine (just the liquid from whatever green olive jar you have on hand)

1 full tsp of coarse-ground black pepper.

INSTRUCTIONS

Mix together and refrigerate in an air-tight container.

SAVED THE LECHWE FOR LAST

On my last day in Africa, I was up early and ready to find a mature red Lechwe. Today, I was using a 7mm mag made by Browning. Despite running into a python as I stalked my prey, and the Leechwe disappeared after I took my shot, I was successful because my tracker was excellent.

RED LECHWE TENDERLOIN
WITH ROSEMARY BALSAMIC REDUCTION

INGREDIENTS

1-1/2 to 2 lb Lechwe tenderloin

2 T of finely chopped parsley leaves

3 T of virgin olive oil

2 garlic cloves, finely chopped

1 T rosemary, finely chopped

INSTRUCTIONS

Mix ingredients in a small bowl, adding salt and pepper to taste. Bring meat to room temperature and cover with mixture. Let the meat sit at room temperature for 30 minutes.

Preheat your oven to 350°F

Place cast iron skillet over high heat, add olive oil and sear meat on each side for 3 minutes or until browned. Remove meat to dish and place in oven for five minutes while you prepare the reduction.

REDUCTION SAUCE

1 T of olive oil
2 T of chopped shallots
1 cup balsamic vinegar
2 T sugar

2 T butter
1 T garlic, chopped
1 large sprig rosemary

INSTRUCTIONS

Using the same skillet without cleaning, add olive oil and shallots and cook until translucent, about one minute then add garlic and cook until tender. Add balsamic vinegar, and 1 large Rosemary sprig and bring to boil. Reduce the vinegar until only 1/4 cup remains. Remove from heat and add 2 T of butter. Stir until melted.

Drizzle sauce over tenderloin and serve.

RED LECHWE, SAGE AND GARLIC SAUSAGE

INGREDIENTS

1 lbs bacon

1-2 lbs ground Lechwe

2 T diced garlic

1 T salt

1/2 tsp mustard powder

1/2 tsp ground black pepper

1 tsp minced fresh sage

3-4 ft pork sausage casing, washed out

4 pieces of bread

INSTRUCTIONS

Grind the bacon using the medium sized grinder plate, then mix all of the ingredients, except the bread and casing, together. When mixed, grind using medium-sized grinder plate. Place mixture in the freezer for 15-20 minutes.

Install sausage tube on the meat grinder, then thread casing onto the sausage tube. Add mixture to grinder and push until it appears at the end of the tube. Pull a portion of the casing past the tube opening and knot the casing. Pull back the casing snug to the tube

Use one hand to allow the casing to slowly slide off of the tube as you feed the mixture with the other hand. You want to prevent air bubbles from forming. Feed the mixture into the casing until all meat is gone.

Feed chunks of bread into the casing until the meat has filled the casing. Remove the casing from the tube, and squeeze bread from casing. Knot casing snuggly against meat. Cut the casing near the knot.

Bring your grill to medium high heat and cook for 15-20 minutes, flipping occasionally.

John McAteer

THE JOURNEY SERIES — BOOK 1

THE JOURNEY

Hunting the World,
A Lifetime of Dreams Fulfilled,
and My Love of the Outdoors

John McAteer

Legends
of The Outdoors

**National
Hall of Famer**

Available at Amazon

Barnes & Noble

& online bookstores

THE JOURNEY SERIES — BOO

THE DARK CONTINEN

John McAteer

CONTACT INFO:

HUNTHARDHUNTSAFE@gmail.com